MEXICAN-AMERICAN WAR

SWATI WADHWANI

ISBN 979-888530144-2

Contents

CHAPTER ONE

Mexican–American War

The Mexican–American War, also known in the United States as the Mexican War and in Mexico as the Intervención estadounidense en México (U.S. intervention in Mexico), was an armed conflict between the United States and Mexico from 1846 to 1848. It followed the 1845 U.S. annexation of Texas, which Mexico considered Mexican territory since the Mexican government did not recognize the Velasco treaty signed by Mexican General Antonio López de Santa Anna when he was a prisoner of the Texian Army during the 1836 Texas Revolution. The Republic of Texas was de facto an independent country, but most of its citizens wished to be annexed by the United States. Domestic sectional politics in the U.S. were preventing annexation since Texas would have been a slave state, upsetting the balance of power between Northern free states and Southern slave states. In the 1844 United States presidential election, Democrat James K. Polk was elected on a platform of expanding U.S. territory in Oregon and Texas. Polk advocated expansion by either peaceful means or by armed force, with the 1845 annexation of Texas furthering that goal by peaceful means. However, the boundary between Texas and Mexico was disputed, with the Republic of Texas and the U.S. asserting it to be the Rio Grande River and Mexico claiming it to be the more-northern Nueces River. Both Mexico and the U.S. claimed the disputed area and sent troops. Polk sent U.S. Army troops to the area; he also sent a diplomatic mission to Mexico to try to negotiate the sale of territory. U.S. troops' presence was designed to lure Mexico into starting the conflict, putting the onus on Mexico and allowing Polk to argue to Congress that a declaration of war should be issued. Mexican forces attacked U.S. forces, and the United States Congress declared war.

Beyond the disputed area of Texas, U.S. forces quickly occupied the regional capital of Santa Fe de Nuevo México along the upper Rio Grande, which had trade relations with the U.S. via the Santa Fe Trail between Missouri and New Mexico. U.S. forces also moved against the province of Alta California and then moved south. The Pacific Squadron of the U.S. Navy blockaded the Pacific coast farther south in the lower Baja California Territory. The Mexican government refused to be pressured into signing a peace treaty at this point, making the U.S. invasion of the Mexican heartland under Major General Winfield Scott and its capture of the capital Mexico City a strategy to force peace negotiations. Although Mexico was defeated on the battlefield, politically its government's negotiating a treaty remained a fraught issue, with some factions refusing to consider any recognition of its loss of territory. Although Polk formally relieved his peace envoy, Nicholas Trist, of his post as negotiator, Trist ignored the order and successfully concluded the 1848 Treaty of Guadalupe Hidalgo. It ended the war, and Mexico recognized the Mexican Cession, areas not part of disputed Texas but conquered by the U.S. Army. These were northern territories of Alta California and Santa Fe de Nuevo México. The U.S. agreed to pay $15 million for the physical damage of the war and assumed $3.25 million of debt already owed by the Mexican government to U.S. citizens. Mexico acknowledged the loss of what became the State of Texas and accepted the Rio Grande as its northern border with the United States.

The victory and territorial expansion Polk envisioned inspired patriotism among some sections of the United States, but the war and treaty drew fierce criticism for the casualties, monetary cost, and heavy-handedness, particularly early on. The question of how to treat the new acquisitions also intensified the debate over slavery in the United States. Although the Wilmot Proviso that explicitly forbade the extension of slavery into conquered Mexican territory was not adopted by Congress, debates about it heightened sectional tensions. Some scholars see the Mexican–American War as leading to the American Civil War, with many officers trained at West Point, who saw action in Mexico, playing prominent leadership roles on each side during the conflict.

In Mexico, the war worsened domestic political turmoil. Since the war was fought on home ground, Mexico suffered a large loss of life of both its soldiers and its civilian population. The nation's financial foundations were undermined, the territory was lost, and national prestige left it in what a group of Mexican writers including Ramón Alcaraz and José María del Castillo Velasco [es] called a "state of degradation and ruin... [As for] the true origin of the war, it is sufficient to say that the insatiable ambition of the United States, favored by our weakness, caused it."

Mexico after independence

Mexico obtained independence from the Spanish Empire with the Treaty of Córdoba in 1821 after a decade of conflict between the royal army and insurgents for independence, with no foreign intervention. The conflict ruined the silver-mining districts of Zacatecas and Guanajuato, so that Mexico began as a sovereign nation with its future financial stability from its main export destroyed. Mexico briefly experimented with monarchy, but became a republic in 1824. This government was characterized by instability, leaving it ill-prepared for a major international conflict when war broke out with the U.S. in 1846. Mexico had successfully resisted Spanish attempts to reconquer its former colony in the 1820s and resisted the French in the so-called Pastry War of 1838, but the secessionists' success in Texas and the Yucatan against the centralist government of Mexico showed the weakness of the Mexican government, which changed hands multiple times. The Mexican military and the Catholic Church in Mexico, both privileged institutions with conservative political views, were stronger politically than the Mexican state.

CHAPTER TWO

U.S. expansionism

Since the early 19th century, the U.S. sought to expand its territory. Jefferson's Louisiana Purchase from France in 1803 gave Spain and the U.S. an undefined border. The young and weak U.S. fought the War of 1812 with Britain, with the U.S. launching an unsuccessful invasion of British Canada and Britain launching an equally unsuccessful counter-invasion. Some boundary issues were solved between the U.S. and Spain with the Adams-Onis Treaty of 1818. U.S. negotiator John Quincy Adams wanted clear possession of East Florida and establishment of U.S. claims above the 42nd parallel, while Spain sought to limit U.S. expansion into what is now the American Southwest. The U.S. then sought to purchase territory from Mexico, starting in 1825. U.S. President Andrew Jackson made a sustained effort to acquire northern Mexican territory, with no success.

Historian Peter Guardino states that in the war "the greatest advantage the United States had was its prosperity." Economic prosperity contributed to political stability in the U.S. Unlike Mexico's financial precariousness, the U.S. was a prosperous country with major resource endowments that Mexico lacked. Its war of independence had taken place generations earlier and was a relatively short conflict that ended with French intervention on the side of the 13 colonies. After independence, the U.S. grew rapidly and expanded westward, marginalizing and displacing Native Americans as settlers cleared land and established farms. With the Industrial Revolution across the Atlantic increasing the demand for cotton for textile factories, there was a large external market of a valuable commodity produced by slave labor in the southern states. This demand helped fuel expansion into northern Mexico. Although there were political conflicts in the U.S., they were largely contained by the framework of the constitution and did not result in revolution or rebellion by 1846, but rather by sectional political conflicts. The expansionism of the U.S. was driven in part by the need to acquire new territory for economic reasons, in particular, as cotton exhausted the soil in areas of the south, new lands had to be brought under cultivation to supply the demand for it. Northerners in the U.S. sought to develop the country's existing resources and expand the industrial sector without expanding the nation's territory. The existing balance of sectional interests would be disrupted by the expansion of slavery into new territory. The Democratic Party strongly supported expansion, so it is not by chance that the U.S. went to war with Mexico under Democratic President James K. Polk.

CHAPTER THREE

Instability in northern Mexico

Neither colonial Mexico nor the newly sovereign Mexican state effectively controlled Mexico's far north and west. Mexico's military and diplomatic capabilities declined after it attained independence from Spain in 1821 and left the northern one-half of the country vulnerable to attacks by Comanche, Apache, and Navajo Native Americans. The Comanche, in particular, took advantage of the weakness of the Mexican state to undertake large-scale raids hundreds of miles into the country to acquire livestock for their own use and to supply an expanding market in Texas and the U.S.

The northern area of Mexico was sparsely settled because of its climate and topography. It was mainly desert with little rainfall so that sedentary agriculture never developed there during the pre-Hispanic or colonial periods. During the colonial era (1521–1821) it had not been well controlled politically. After independence, Mexico contended with internal struggles that sometimes verged on civil war, and the situation on the northern frontier was not a high priority for the government in central Mexico. In northern Mexico, the end of Spanish rule was marked by the end of financing for presidios and for gifts to Native Americans to maintain the peace. The Comanche and Apache were successful in raiding for livestock and looting much of northern Mexico outside the scattered cities. The raids after 1821 resulted in the death of many Mexicans, halted most transportation and communications, and decimated the ranching industry that was a mainstay of the northern economy. As a result, the demoralized civilian population of northern Mexico put up little resistance to the invading U.S. army.

Distance and hostile activity from Native Americans also made communications and trade between the heartland of Mexico and provinces such as Alta California and New Mexico difficult. As a result, New Mexico was dependent on the overland Santa Fe Trail trade with the United States at the outbreak of the war.

The Mexican government's policy of settlement of U.S. citizens in its province of Tejas was aimed at expanding control into Comanche lands, the Comancheria. But, instead of settling in the dangerous central and western parts of the province, people settled in East Texas, which held rich farmland contiguous to the southern U.S. slave states. As settlers poured in from the U.S., the Mexican government discouraged further settlement with its 1829 abolition of slavery.

CHAPTER FOUR

Texas revolution, republic, and U.S. annexation

In 1800, Spain's colonial province of Texas (Tejas) had few inhabitants, with only about 7,000 non-Indian settlers. The Spanish crown developed a policy of colonization to more effectively control the territory. After independence, the Mexican government implemented the policy, granting Moses Austin, a banker from Missouri, a large tract of land in Texas. Austin died before he could bring his plan of recruiting American settlers for the land to fruition, but his son, Stephen F. Austin, brought over 300 American families into Texas. This started the steady trend of migration from the United States into the Texas frontier. Austin's colony was the most successful of several colonies authorized by the Mexican government. The Mexican government intended the new settlers to act as a buffer between the Tejano residents and the Comanches, but the non-Hispanic colonists tended to settle in areas with decent farmland and trade connections with Louisiana rather than farther west where they would have been an effective buffer against the Indians.

In 1829, because of the large influx of American immigrants, the non-Hispanic outnumbered native Spanish speakers in Texas. President Vicente Guerrero, a hero of Mexican independence, moved to gain more control over Texas and its influx of non-Hispanic colonists from the southern U.S. and discourage further immigration by abolishing slavery in Mexico. The Mexican government also decided to reinstate the property tax and increase tariffs on shipped American goods. The settlers and many Mexican businessmen in the region rejected the demands, which led to Mexico closing Texas to additional immigration, which continued from the United States into Texas illegally.

In 1834, Mexican conservatives seized the political initiative, and General Antonio López de Santa Anna became the centralist president of Mexico. The conservative-dominated Congress abandoned the federal system, replacing it with a unitary central government that removed power from the states. Leaving politics to those in Mexico City, General Santa Anna led the Mexican army to quash the semi-independence of Texas. He had done that in Coahuila (in 1824, Mexico had merged Texas and Coahuila into the enormous state of Coahuila y Tejas). Austin called Texians to arms and they declared independence from Mexico in 1836. After Santa Anna defeated the Texians in the Battle of the Alamo, he was defeated by the Texian Army commanded by General Sam Houston and was captured at the Battle of San Jacinto; he signed a treaty with Texas President David Burnet to allow Texas to plead its case for independence with the Mexican government but did not commit himself or Mexico to anything beyond that. He negotiated under duress and as a captive, and therefore had no standing to commit Mexico to a treaty. The Mexican Congress did not ratify it. Although Mexico did not recognize Texas independence, Texas consolidated its status as an independent republic and received official recognition from Britain, France, and the United States, which all advised Mexico not to try to reconquer the new nation. Most Texians wanted to join the United States, but the annexation of Texas was contentious in the U.S. Congress, where Whigs and Abolitionists were largely opposed, although neither group went so far as to deny funds for the war.:150–155 In 1845, Texas agreed to the offer of annexation by the U.S. Congress and became the 28th state on December 29, 1845, which set the stage for the conflict with Mexico.